the guide to owning a
Water Dragon

John Coborn

T.F.H. Publications, Inc.
One TFH Plaza
Third and Union Avenues
Neptune City, NJ 07753

This book has been published with the intent to provide accurate and authoritative information in regard to the subject matter within. While every precaution has been taken in preparation of this book, the publisher and author assume no responsibility for errors or omissions. Neither is any liability assumed for damages resulting from the use of the information herein.

ISBN 0-7938-0281-4

Contents

The enlarged, white conical scales behind the jaws of a green water dragon, *Physignathus cocincinus*, are a trademark of the species regardless of age.

THE GUIDE TO OWNING A WATER DRAGON

Introduction

Water dragons, sailfin lizards, and basilisks—what a combination! For a person with a fanatic interest in lizards, such exotic names bring to mind thoughts of steamy jungles and mountain streams littered with giant, moss-covered boulders.

I was around nine years old when I first became aware of such exotic creatures. All three groups fascinated me. Perhaps they reminded me of the days of the dinosaurs, when reptiles ruled the earth. Indeed, if you look at a few artist's impressions of what various dinosaurs looked like, some of them bear more than a vague resemblance to many of our modern lizards. My interests in reptiles led me to keeping many of them in my home over the years, and I eventually became a curator of reptiles in a zoological institution. Most of my early information was gleaned from the few books that were around at the time and from various articles and papers that appeared in scientific herpetological journals.

Adult green water dragons are gentle, tame pets.

The green basilisk, *Basiliscus plumifrons*, belongs to the family Corytophanidae, a close relative of the iguanas and anoles.

In contrast, sailfin dragons (here the green or Weber's form) and water dragons belong to the family Agamidae, close relatives of the chameleons.

Though they lack bright colors, brown water dragons, *Physignathus lesueuri*, are similar in most respects to green water dragons and also are bred in captivity.

During the last 10 or 15 years, however, growing interest in herpetology has led to an increase of literature concerning reptiles and amphibians and how to efficiently keep them in captivity. Water dragons and basilisks (and to some extent sailfin lizards) are appearing more regularly on the market, and, though they cannot be described as the easiest of reptiles to keep, their very appearance puts them in great demand. With ongoing enthusiasm and good husbandry practices, there is no reason why any hobbyist should fail in keeping and breeding these fascinating creatures.

Why have we lumped these three distinctive lizard groups into a single volume? The connection is in their habitats and modes of life. All are tropical to subtropical, and all need large bodies of water. This means, of course, that captive specimens require similar care and housing.

This book is intended to present information on the care and breeding of water dragons, basilisks, and sailfin lizards. It contains all the necessary information needed by a determined hobbyist to get started in this challenging aspect of the terrarium hobby. By being a responsible keeper of any or all of these fascinating lizards, you too can play a role in their continued survival.

Though baby green water dragons are commonly available, this lizard does not make a really good pet until at least half-grown.

THE GUIDE TO OWNING A WATER DRAGON

Water Dragons

The water dragons, two species of the genus *Physignathus*, are members of the Old World lizard family known as the Agamidae. This group contains perhaps as many as 350 to 400 species in 45 to 50 genera.

The most commonly seen water dragon in captivity is the Green Water Dragon (sometimes referred to as the Chinese Water Dragon), *Physignathus cocincinus*. There is only one other species somewhat questionably referred to this genus, the much less spectacular but often available Brown Water Dragon, *Physignathus lesueuri*, of Australia. Both the Green and the Brown Water Dragons will be covered in detail in this chapter.

GREEN WATER DRAGON
PHYSIGNATHUS COCINCINUS

Green Water Dragons are relatively large and are somewhat reminiscent of American Green Iguanas, *Iguana iguana*, in general appearance. They are regularly imported from several areas of Southeast Asia, especially Vietnam and southern China. Once regularly collected in Thailand, they are now at least somewhat protected in that country.

This familiar water dragon is one of the more adaptable pet lizards. They are colorful, usually easy to handle, do not grow excessively large, settle well into captivity, and, given the right conditions, will breed in captivity. Being of moderate size, their housing needs can be met, so they can even be kept in apartments. Green Water Dragons also are unlikely to destroy terrarium plants.

Description

The robust, slightly laterally compressed (flattened from side to side) body is generally a lush green in color with three to five wide dark oblique bands on the side. There are touches of pink and blue around the throat and often a yellowish wash along

This female (low crests, pale lips) green water dragon is easy to handle—a baby would be nervous and difficult to touch.

the flanks. The tail is banded with dark brown and pale green or whitish. Some individuals are distinctly blue on the body. Both sexes sport a spiny crest that runs from the back of the head to well onto the tail, broken over the hind legs. Adult males have a somewhat higher and more spectacular nuchal (neck) crest than the females, and the individual spines are longer. The limbs are well-developed (the back legs especially long, though slender) with sharp-clawed fingers and toes. The eyes are relatively large, the irises typically bright orange. Two or three enlarged white, conical spines behind the angles of the jaws are typical of the species. Maximum length, including the tail, is about 3 feet in adult males. Females are somewhat shorter and more slightly built than are males. The strongly laterally compressed tail makes up over two-thirds of the entire length.

Sex Determination

Juvenile Green Water Dragons are diffi-cult to sex, but adults—animals at least 18 months old—can be determined when adequate comparative knowledge is available. The adult males have larger heads and more robust jowls, generally with brighter colors and more aggressive behavior. Both sexes have a row of femoral pores along the inner surfaces of the thighs, but in the males these are much larger. Sexually active males appear to secrete a waxy substance from the pores that leaves scent trails for females to follow and marks male territories.

Natural Range

This is a species that appears to be restricted to mainland Southeast Asia, where it is recorded from Burma, Thailand, Malaysia, Cambodia, Vietnam, and southeastern China. Reports from Indonesian islands may be based on introduced or transshipped specimens.

Habitat and Habits

The Green Water Dragon typically is found in riverine evergreen forests, where

The narrow pale bands on the back of a green water dragon are not always visible in adults.

it stays close to water. An arboreal lizard, it often frequents foliage overhanging water, into which it will drop and take refuge when threatened. It is an accomplished swimmer, propelling itself through the water with lateral undulations of its flattened tail while holding its limbs close to its body. To avoid predators it will submerge itself, coming up for air among vegetation and only returning to the land when the offending creature has gone. It also is quite at home on the ground and can show amazing speed when escaping enemies or chasing prey. It often runs on its hind limbs for short distances, much like some basilisks and much smaller desert lizards. The Green Water Dragon feeds on a variety of invertebrates, small frogs, lizards, and nestling birds. Only occasionally will it show herbivorous tendencies in nature.

Green Water Dragons can be regarded as semi-gregarious, often living in groups of one dominant adult male and several adult females. Juveniles tend to be more solitary and secretive. The dominant male is territorial and will defend his area without hesitation. Several territories may be found within view of each other, each dominant male advertising his presence by frequent head-bobbing. Any subordinate males are driven off, but violent fighting is rare. (The jaws and teeth can inflict painful, even mortal, bites to invaders.) When actively engaged in defending his territory or when in breeding condition, the colors of the dominant male are greatly enhanced. Juveniles are nervous and aggressive, not very social.

Reproduction in the Wild

Green Water Dragons are ready to breed by the time they are about two

Adult green water dragons often are quite social, bunching up under a basking light and sharing a feeding dish. Babies, on the other hand, may be aggressive.

THE GUIDE TO OWNING A WATER DRAGON

The bright peachy patch over the front legs as well as the bright throat are signs of adulthood in this probable female green water dragon.

This breeding male green water dragon has bright pink tints on the lips and a very high nuchal crest typical of his sex.

years old. At this age the males will be about 27 inches in total length and females about 24 inches. Smaller males rarely breed because they are driven from the females by the larger dominant males. The breeding response is influenced by climatic conditions. Green Water Dragons from Thailand, for instance, are probably influenced by photoperiod (length of daylight), temperature, and, to a lesser extent, humidity. There is a winter dry season (December and January) and a drop in temperature to not less than 65°F. Mating usually occurs at the end of the dry season, when the temperature begins to rise and the hours of daylight increase. This strategy is designed so that eggs have optimum warmth and moisture during their development. Eight to 12 eggs are laid in a shallow burrow in damp soil, often close to the water's edge but above the high water mark.

Captive Reproduction

Most reptile species are unable to completely adapt to conditions alien to those of their native habitat. While they may survive for a short time in an artificial environment, they are most unlikely to breed unless you provide more familiar conditions. If you do this, however, you should have fewer problems getting your Green Water Dragons to breed. For breeding, you should select only healthy, well-fed specimens that are a minimum of two years old and 24 inches in total length.

You can keep one adult male with up to three females. For a period of two months during the latter part of winter (say January and February), reduce the photoperiod to only ten hours per day, the ambient daytime temperature to around 77°F, and the ambient nighttime temperature to around 70°F. During this two-month rest period, feeding should be

Looking at this pair of adult green water dragons in excellent color, is there any doubt why hobbyists are willing to give this species the cage room and detailed attention it demands?

Because these are very active lizards and hard to capture, few dealers can get adult green water dragons in perfect physical shape. Notice the tear on the tail and the skinned knee—both may heal if the lizard is given proper veterinary and terrarium care.

reduced to once per week, with the food offered around midday.

During the last week of the cooling period, gradually increase the length of day and the temperature to return to the summer schedule. Also begin the feeding routine again. After the climate and feeding strategy have been "normalized," breeding activity should begin. This will consist of much head-bobbing by the male, who will chase the females around in an attempt to arouse them. A receptive female eventually will allow the male to seize her by the nuchal (neck) crest and will raise her tail to allow the male to twist his body beneath hers in order to insert a hemipenis. Copulation may take up to 30 minutes.

Like other larger lizards, mating can be rough, and it is not uncommon for females to come away with small scratches as well as bite marks on the neck and head. These seldom cause problems and do not need treatment unless you notice they are obviously infected. If healthy and kept well, water dragons show a remarkable resilience to small wounds.

Oviposition and Egg Development

Once fertilized, the eggs will develop in the gravid female for a period of about 60 days. Toward the end of this period, the female often will eat less food and prefer smaller prey items, sometimes refusing all food in the final week before oviposition (egg-laying). After about four weeks of gestation the eggs will become apparent in the plumpness of the mother's body, and later the actual outlines of the eggs will be observed against the skin of the abdomen.

Young green water dragons may be difficult to care for and require careful attention to all details of their environment.

THE GUIDE TO OWNING A WATER DRAGON

Though the specimens usually seen are just shades of brown, adult brown water dragons in breeding color may have delightful touches of pink and blue on the head and over the legs.

You can prepare an egg-laying site for the female by providing a mixture of moist peat and sand in a layer about 9 inches deep. If you place a flat object like a piece of slate or a board over the layer, the female most likely will start to burrow under its edge. The 8 to 12 white, leathery shelled eggs are about an inch in diameter and are laid in a chamber at the base of the burrow.

Incubation

After oviposition has occurred and the female has left the burrow, the eggs usually are immediately removed for artificial incubation because conditions in the terrarium will not be suitable for a normal incubation process. (Females give no care to their eggs and young, so you are not depriving the eggs of natural care.) Handle the eggs with care and keep them in the position in which they were laid for at least the first three days. Unlike the eggs of birds, which are turned regularly, reptile eggs should not be turned; turned eggs, at least early in incubation, may result in embryos "suffocated" in the yolk. It is advisable to carefully mark the upper surface of the egg (as laid) with a non-toxic wax pen; felt-tipped markers may be toxic.

The eggs are placed in an incubation container that can consist of a simple closed plastic box with a few small holes drilled into the lid to allow for free circulation of fresh air. Most reptile breeders now consider granular vermiculite (an inert, absorbent, mineral insulating material) to be by far the best incubation substrate. The

Green water dragons have been bred repeatedly both in zoos and by hobbyists. Maintain the proper humidity and temperature to assure successful incubation of the eggs.

THE GUIDE TO OWNING A WATER DRAGON

Unlike green water dragons, brown water dragons are quite variable over their eastern Australian range, with several subspecies recognized by specialists.

amount of vermiculite used is mixed with a similar amount (by weight) of water (preferably distilled rather than treated tap water) so that it is moist but not soggy; the vermiculite should adhere into a loose ball when squeezed in your fist. The eggs are buried with their top third exposed. They then are covered with a thin, loose layer of moistened natural sphagnum moss, which can be easily removed for inspection of the eggs.

State of the art incubators for almost any kind of egg are available on the market, ranging from simple devices to complicated electronically controlled machines, and come in a variety of price ranges. However, I have experienced success with many lizard eggs by using a simple, homemade incubator. The box holding the eggs is placed on two bricks at the bottom of a thick-walled Styrofoam ice chest or box (such as used to cool beer or ship tropical fishes) containing about 2 inches of water. In the water is a good submersible heater with wiring leading to a reliable thermostat. There also should be a good thermometer in the water (preferably electronic). The heater is started about two days before the eggs are going into the incubator to allow it to reach a stable incubation temperature. The warm, moist air in the incubator, which is kept closed, simulates natural conditions.

During incubation the eggs will absorb moisture, take in oxygen, and release carbon dioxide. It thus is imperative that the air in the incubator remains moist but is not allowed to stagnate. Allow a complete air change twice a week by removing the lid for a few minutes. The relatively warm air in the container will rise into the atmosphere and will be replaced by new, cooler air that will quickly warm up, providing the lid is not left off for too long. Should the incubation medium appear to be drying out, an occasional light misting spray of water on the surface will rectify the situation. However, you must be careful to avoid spraying the eggs themselves, for this could easily spoil them.

Incubation takes between 60 and 70 days, depending on temperature. Incubation at a temperature slightly lower than the norm will be longer, while a temperature slightly higher will shorten the period. It is wise to try and keep as close as possible to the recommended temperature of 85°F throughout the incubation period.

When hatching time approaches, you must inspect the eggs frequently. The hatchling will slit the egg shell with its egg tooth in order to escape. Individual hatchlings may take anywhere from 6 to 24 hours to leave the eggs, depending on how long it takes to finish absorbing the yolk sac and allow the lungs to function fully. All fertile, fully developed eggs should have hatched within about 48 hours of the first pipping.

Rearing Hatchlings

Allow hatchlings to completely free themselves from the egg shells before attempting to handle them. They will still have the yolk sac attached to the belly and must be allowed to fully absorb its contents. As soon as the hatchlings are free they may be moved to separate rearing quarters. They require vitamin and calcium supplements on their food.

BROWN WATER DRAGON
PHYSIGNATHUS LESUEURI

Though usually tougher to obtain than the Green Water Dragon, this species, sometimes called the Australian Water Dragon, also makes an excellent terrarium pet. Its scarcity in captivity undoubtedly revolves on the Australian government's policy of not allowing any native animals to be exported. Indeed, even in Australia itself native herpetologists often find it difficult to obtain specimens. However, there are a small number of breeders of this species in Europe and North America, and they produce just about enough specimens to supply the demand. At the moment, all wild-caught Brown Water Dragons sold in the U.S. should be considered contraband. Incidentally, some herpetologists feel this species should not be placed in *Physignathus* but instead should be in its own genus or with *Hypsilurus*, the forest dragons.

Description

Brown Water Dragons are similar in general shape to the Green Water Dragon but may grow slightly longer, with a maximum head to tail-tip length of almost 40 inches, of which at least two-thirds is taken up by the tail. Adult females are somewhat shorter and of slighter build than males. The nuchal crest is less prominent in this species. The general color is gray to gray-brown above, usually with a series of dark brownish and whitish bands along the body and tail. Generally there is a wide black band back from the eye. Many individuals are suffused with red (males) or pale tan (females) on the throat and anterior surface of the abdomen. Sexually mature males often sport combinations of red, blue, green, and yellow, especially on the throat and chest. The underside generally is yellowish brown with darker blotching on the chest.

Sex Determination

As in the Green Water Dragon, males are larger and more robust than females, and they also tend to carry more color. Females lack red on the chest and have few indications of femoral pores.

Natural Range

Brown Water Dragons are confined to eastern Australia, following the mountain ranges and coastal strip from eastern Victoria through New South Wales and Queensland to Cape York at the northeastern tip of the continent. Records from New Guinea are based on a misidentification as well as specimens smuggled from Australia; the species does not occur naturally on New Guinea.

Habitat and Habits

Usually found close to creeks, rivers, and estuaries, this semiaquatic and arboreal (tree-climbing) lizard frequents trees and rocky areas, taking refuge in the water when disturbed. It often is found close to human habitation, becoming relatively fearless after prolonged contact with people. A colony once lived near a famous Queensland casino, the lizards sometimes taking an occasional dip in the swimming pool! Further habits and behaviors are similar to those described for the Green Water Dragon.

Captive Reproduction

In the broad sense, Brown Water Dragons can be bred much like Green Water Dragons. Somewhat cooler temperatures are recommended during the two-month winter rest period, however: daytime, 70°F, nighttime, 60°F. The Brown Water Dragon lays a clutch of 6 to 16 eggs in a burrow dug by the female near water but not in her normal territory. The eggs are collected and incubated much as described earlier. Hatching may take 70 to 100 days.

The green or Weber's sailfin, *Hydrosaurus* species, may be one of the most spectacularly colored large lizards available to hobbyists. It apparently is undescribed.

Sailfin Lizards

Sailfin lizards are at present less often available than are water dragons and also are relatively more difficult to maintain. Breeding successes are not very common, but further research may eventually reverse this situation. Sailfins undoubtedly are a challenge even to the more advanced herpetoculturist. Two or three species are known. From the Philippines comes the most commonly seen species, *Hydrosaurus pustulatus*, the Philippine Sailfin, while the Indonesian Sailfin, Soa Soa, or Lassara, *Hydrosaurus amboinensis*, comes from the eastern islands of Indonesia, including Irian Jaya on western New Guinea. It is likely that these two names represent either variation in a single species or a complex of several very similar forms. Regardless, hobbyists (and herpetologists) cannot be expected to distinguish the two. The commonly seen name *Hydrosaurus weberi* technically represents a synonym of *H. amboinensis*; the distinctive green sailfins sold under this name (from Indonesia) may represent an undescribed species.

Sailfins have a more nervous disposition than do water dragons and should therefore be housed in a quiet situation and disturbed as little as possible. Regular handling tends to tame them somewhat, but a tame animal is less likely to breed. Sailfins require more vegetable matter in their diet than do water dragons, and adults require a 50/50 animal-vegetable diet. Chopped mixed fruits and vegetables in as big a variety as possible are recommended. All the species require similar husbandry.

PHILIPPINE SAILFIN
HYDROSAURUS PUSTULATUS
Description
A large, robust agamid, this lizard has a slightly laterally compressed body and a broad, flattened tail, powerful limbs, and

strong claws. The adult male, which can reach a maximum length of 47 inches, carries a spectacular spiny nuchal (neck) crest that continues along the back as a tall "sail" supported by the vertebrae. This sail is absent or only vestigial in the females. The head is relatively long and the snout upturned. In the male the snout is somewhat bulbous and embellished with a number of small spines. The toes are edged with narrow, scaly flaps of skin used in the lizard's aquatic activities.

The ground color is brown to olive with a number of darker bands along the body and tail. Excited males take on lighter hues, often becoming suffused with ocher yellow or bright blue on the head.

Sex Determination

Juvenile males begin to develop the tail crest at an age of about six months. Adult males, generally somewhat larger than the females, are unmistakable with their tall tail crests. The males also exhibit enlarged femoral pores.

Natural Range

Many of the islands in the Philippine chain, though apparently absent from Palawan.

Habitat and Habits

Sailfin lizards always are associated with water, often living in thickly wooded areas close to rivers and basking on tree limbs overhanging the water. They also may be found in rocky areas, where they bask on boulders in streams, the dominant male taking the highest vantage point, surrounded by females and juveniles on lesser boulders. Such family groups may be found at regular intervals along watercourses in suitable areas. Young sailfins, like basilisks, are able to run for short distances on the water surface, though larger specimens are no

This adult male Philippine sailfin, *Hydrosaurus pustulatus*, displays striking blue tints over much of the head and front legs.

THE GUIDE TO OWNING A WATER DRAGON

Most sailfins seen in captivity are shades of brown and often unhealthy. Hobbyists have not yet discovered how to keep these lizards truly happy in the terrarium.

The gigantic hind feet of sailfins, with the toes broadly fringed with modified scales to help when swimming, are a fascinating adaptation for an aquatic environment.

longer able to do this due to their bulk. All sailfins are excellent swimmers, entering the water to escape predators (primarily birds of prey) or to pursue prey.

Reproduction in the Wild

Little has been documented on the wild breeding habits of any of the sailfins, though there is some evidence to suggest they are similar to those of water dragons. They do lay their eggs in nests dug in soil near their home streams.

Captive Reproduction

Though not as prolifically bred as water dragons or basilisks, the propagation of sailfins is making some progress. Regular importations of Philippine Sailfins unfortunately appear to be detrimental to a cap-

tive-breeding breakthrough rather than an encouragement. Wild-caught specimens sell for much lower prices than captive-breds, so a non-import market is never able to develop. It is ironic to have to say that this is just one example of how wild stocks can be seriously depleted just because they are initially available in reasonable numbers in the wild. Here we are reminded of the days when it was a case of "if it dies, we can just buy another one." It is extremely important that more captive-breeding programs are initiated now before the situation deteriorates.

Both male and female sailfins are exceedingly territorial. In captivity it rarely is possible to give a group of animals enough room for each individual to possess its own "turf." It therefore is suggested that only a single pair of adults be kept together in the same terrarium, the size of which should not be less than 6 feet in length, 4 feet high, and 4 feet wide. Another method is to keep each specimen individually, only introducing males to females at breeding time after a short rest period at reduced temperature and photoperiod as described for Green Water Dragons. This pre-breeding conditioning is best carried out in mid-winter, with mating in early spring. Only specimens two or more years old and in good health should be used for breeding. Mating behavior is similar to that described for Green Water Dragons, with the male grabbing the nuchal crest of the female in his mouth before copulation.

Oviposition

Once fertilized, the gravid female will lay her eggs some 60 days later. It is best to provide her with an egg-laying box, preferably a large plastic container with a deep layer of moist sphagnum moss or vermiculite. A hole large enough to allow the female to enter is cut into the side of the container, the bottom of the hole being level with the substrate layer. She usually will find her own way into the container and lay her 6 to 12 eggs. Larger, older females usually will lay a greater number of eggs per clutch than younger specimens.

Incubation

Similar to that described for Green Water Dragons. An incubation temperature of 83 to 86°F is recommended.

Almost all sailfins available to hobbyists are young, and almost all are wild-caught. This makes them difficult to acclimate to the terrarium.

All the trials of keeping a young sailfin healthy are forgotten when it matures to display full color and fin development.

Rearing the Hatchlings

Hatchling sailfins require high humidity. To avoid desiccation they should be wetted daily with a mist sprayer. They should be fed on small invertebrates at first—mealworms, crickets, etc.—that have been dusted with a vitamin/mineral powder, then at about four months of age offered finely chopped fruits and vegetables. At three months they can be offered pinkie mice. The youngsters should be housed separately as soon as they start to exhibit territorial behavior, which can be as early as six months.

Basilisks

Basilisks (family Corytophanidae) are totally unrelated to the water dragons and sailfins (family Agamidae), but they have somewhat similar habits and captive needs and are no less spectacular. Given the right conditions, basilisks will thrive in the terrarium and are not too difficult to breed. At the present time, much research is going into the captive propagation of two species, and it seems that these will be readily available to hobbyists in the near future.

The name basilisk is derived from the Greek "*basiliskos*" and is based on the legend of a fabulous beast from the Middle Ages that resembled a cross between a dragon and a rooster. Basilisks formerly were included in the family Iguanidae, but recent taxonomic activity now has placed the genus *Basiliscus* in the family Corytophanidae, a step not recognized by all herpetologists.

BROWN BASILISK
BASILISCUS BASILISCUS
Description

This slender lizard reaches a maximum length of around 32 inches, of which two-thirds is taken up by the tail. The strong limbs are relatively long and slender, the hind feet with long toes. The animal has an impressive, helmet-like crest on the head,

An adult male *Basiliscus vittatus* from western Mexico.

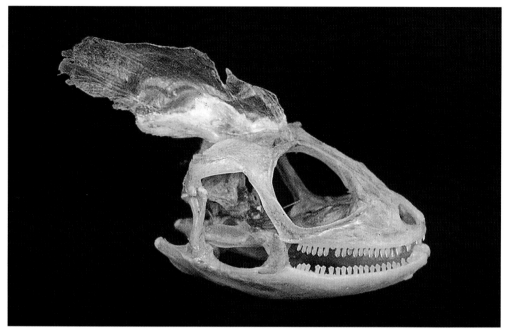
In basilisks the crests are supported by thin bone, as seen in this skull, and are not formed only from scales.

an erectable sail-like crest running along the back, and another crest on the tail. The general color is brown to olive-green and marked with a series of black cross bands along the flanks and dorsal crest. There is a narrow white stripe stretching from the back of the eye along the flank, fading as it reaches the hind limb.

Sex Determination

Females are shorter and more slender than males. The male's crest is conspicuously higher than that of the female.

Natural Range

Brown Basilisks are a species of southern Central America, Costa Rica to Panama, entering South America in northwestern Colombia.

Habitat and Habits

Like the other basilisks, this species inhabits trees and vegetation usually close to permanent water. They all are adept swimmers and divers and are well-known for their ability to run on the surface of the water. This is accomplished by using the scaly flaps of skin between the toes, aided by air pockets formed under the feet when they sink slightly into the water. Individuals have been known to reach speeds of 7.5 miles per hour. Such behavior usually is performed while escaping from predators and inevitably ends in the basilisk sinking below the water surface. Male basilisks are extremely territorial and will not tolerate any other male in their sight. Encounters often result in vicious fights, the victor sometimes inflicting serious wounds on his adversary.

Reproduction in the Wild

Mating and egg-laying are seasonally correlated. Once a female is gravid, she will dig a hole about 4.5 inches deep and

Green basilisks, *Basiliscus plumifrons*, have not only remarkable crests and bright colors, but even the orange eye of the adult is distinctive.

Notice the double crest on the head of this Costa Rican green basilisk and the deep notch between the crests on the back and the tail. In females the crests are all poorly developed.

Basiliscus vittatus is common in Mexico but seldom available. Notice the narrow white or yellow stripe continues well past the front leg in this species.

Brown basilisks, *Basiliscus basiliscus*, often appear dull in color, lacking the long bright stripe of *B. vittatus*. Admittedly, however, some basilisk specimens are difficult to identify based only on coloration.

In this adult male *Basiliscus vittatus* from Panama, the bright stripe is still strong and long, while the head crest is larger and the back crest smaller than in typical brown basilisks.

Care to guess at the identification of this immature basilisk? Notice the absence of a clean white or yellow stripe running from the eye to beyond the front leg. Brown basilisks are occasionally bred in captivity.

THE GUIDE TO OWNING A WATER DRAGON

An immature *Basiliscus vittatus* from Costa Rica displays a stripe running back to the tail as well as a generally more slender look than brown basilisks of similar size.

Some hobbyists recently have had luck with *Basiliscus vittatus*, even to occasional breedings. This is a wild female.

lay around 12 eggs (7 to 18), one after the other, at five-minute intervals. She then turns around and covers up the hole and remains at the site for a short time (perhaps until she is assured of her safety?), then leaves and does not return.

A female *Basiliscus vittatus* has a very small crest.

Captive Reproduction

Since wild basilisks breed only in humid conditions (during the rainy season), it is important to increase humidity if a breeding response is desired. Basilisks kept at a 60% relative humidity will be encouraged to breed when this is increased to 80% or more. An adult male can be kept together with two or three adult females, but *never* keep two or more males together or you will soon end up with only one live specimen or perhaps none at all!

GREEN BASILISK
BASILISCUS PLUMIFRONS
Description

Larger and more robust than the previous species, an adult male can reach a maximum length of about 36 inches, much of this tail. This species is truly spectacular in appearance, the male having a double crest or "plume" on the head, an

Though beautiful and not really difficult to keep under the right conditions, many green basilisks suffer from rotting of the fins, a bacterial (?) disease that may be fatal.

erectable semicircular dorsal crest, and another high crest along the tail. The color usually is a rich leaf-green with rows of whitish spots along the abdomen and dark bands along the dorsal crest. The undersides are yellowish, and the iris is bright orange. Some captive specimens take on an overall bluish tinge. There is some evidence to suggest that the feeding of yellow plant pigments (as in dandelion flowers) will correct this, but many breeders prefer the blue and sell such specimens as color variations.

Sex Determination

The female is somewhat smaller than the male and lacks his spectacular crests.

Natural Range

Green Basilisks are found only in northern Central America, from Guatemala to Costa Rica.

Habitat and Habits

An inhabitant of tropical rain forests, the Green Basilisk is more arboreal than the Brown Basilisk, but it still is adept at running on water.

Reproduction

Reproduction in the wild and captive reproduction are much as described for the Brown Basilisk. Under ideal conditions, captive-bred basilisks will become sexually mature at 18 months of age, though for best results it is recommended that they should not be mated until they are at least two years old.

OTHER SPECIES

Two other species in the genus *Basiliscus* that virtually never turn up in captivity are the Striped Basilisk, *Basiliscus vittatus*, found from southern Mexico to Colombia, and the Large-scaled or Red-headed Basilisk, *B. galeritus*, found (rarely) over a large range from Ecuador and Colombia north through Panama to Costa Rica. Though occasionally imported for the pet hobby, they are hard to find and usually difficult to distinguish from the Brown Basilisk. When available, they can be kept much like the more common species.

Housing Considerations

All lizards discussed in this book require similar captive housing. Rather than repetitively discuss housing for each animal, I will provide general guidelines that can be adjusted as necessary. Whatever type of enclosure is used, you must bear in mind the importance of providing all the necessary life support systems that together produce an environment suitable for your lizards.

CHOOSING AN ENCLOSURE

In general, glass aquaria with secure, ventilated lids are suitable for small juveniles of all the species. A good rule of thumb regarding size is that the length of the tank should be at least twice the length of the lizard being kept in it. Hatchling Green Water Dragons, for instance, are about 6 inches long, so in theory a 12-inch tank is large enough. However, such hatchlings grow rapidly, so it is strongly recommended that you start off with a tank at least 2 feet long, 1 foot wide, and 1 foot high (10-gallon). For subadults and adults, you obviously will require a much larger tank (perhaps impractical for glass aquaria). A minimum size of 6 feet long by 2 feet wide and 3 feet high may be large enough to hold a pair of adult water dragons or basilisks or a single sailfin. Note that the recommended height exceeds that of many standard aquaria.

Such large aquaria can be difficult to service because you will have access only from the top. Additionally, a container with only top ventilation (which describes an aquarium with a screen lid) is less efficient than one with vents in the sides as well as the top. The serious hobbyist usually prefers a custom-built terrarium made with a combination of glass and plexiglass. The glass will provide the main panels, and the plexiglass can be drilled to house ventilation panels or at least rows of holes. A habitat can be constructed with the front

All the lizards in this book need large terraria or cages that are planted (natural or artificial plants) and kept humid and warm. Without these basic needs being met, you cannot successfully keep basilisks or dragons.

and side viewing panels plus the lower half of the rear panel all made of glass. The upper part of the rear panel can be made from a framed, removable sheet of plexiglass into which a number of ventilation holes have been drilled.

Wooden enclosures, with access doors at the front and ventilation panels in the sides, also are very useful and are perhaps easier to make and handle than glass aquaria. They are lighter and usually can be made larger, giving you a greater scope for decoration. All timber used must be coated inside and out with a high-quality, non-toxic, waterproof paint or varnish to prevent rotting. Pressure-treated lumber should be considered to be toxic and not used or completely coated. For very large lizards, many hobbyists use a wooden frame covered with hardware cloth or chicken wire of the appropriate mesh.

A PERMANENT TERRARIUM

One of the most satisfactory ways of displaying your lizards is to build a permanent terrarium in some part of the house. Such a setup can be made of wood, bricks, or cement blocks, with framed glass doors on the front and/or ends. The major advantage of such a terrarium is that you can build a permanent landscape into the base with rocks and include a drainable concrete pond and possibly even a waterfall. You will also be able to conceal all the wires, pipes, etc., for the life support systems by building them in as you go. You may even wish to go a step further and construct a paludarium, which is a combined terrarium and aquarium with both over- and underwater viewing. Such a structure would be ideal for studying the underwater habits of your pets.

THE GUIDE TO OWNING A WATER DRAGON

ENCLOSURE DÉCOR

Décor will vary from the simplest items to those that aid in the creation of naturalistic rainforest landscapes. It is best to aim for a simple setup rather than have an enclosure so cluttered that it is difficult to clean and view the occupants.

Substrates (Bedding)

There are a number of substrate options. Many hobbyists use mixtures of potting soil and coarse sand, but this tends to be messy when the animals are continually entering and leaving the water. A better mixture consists of equal parts of orchid bark and pea shingle. You can buy either of these in many pet shops. The advantage of the bark is that it will retain moisture and thus help keep up humidity within the enclosure. A 2-inch layer will be adequate. Commercially available substrates also may have their advantages but tend to be more expensive.

Climbing and Basking Facilities

Water dragons, basilisks, and sailfins are adept climbers and like to bask on tree limbs over the water. Stout branches can be used. It is interesting to go out and look for bizarrely shaped tree limbs. A good place to search is along the seashore or along rivers that have recently flooded. Here you are likely to find dead branches that have been weathered nicely by the elements. All tree branches used should be scrubbed and disinfected with a 1:19 solution of household bleach and water. Branches should be wired into position in the cage so that they don't fall down and pose a danger to the lizards. Make sure some branches are placed horizontally to provide basking and resting sites.

Rocks also have their uses in large setups. They may be used for climbing and basking and will add to the attractiveness of the display. You can buy rocks in aquarium

Many bedding materials are available for use in the dragon and basilisk habitat. Wood pulp and aspen shavings are especially popular at the moment.

Housing for an adult green basilisk or any other lizard covered here may be difficult because of their size and need for a warm, humid environment.

To keep a sailfin dragon healthy, you need not only a large terrarium or cage, but also a pool for bathing, swimming, and psychological well-being.

shops or go out and collect your own. Like the tree branches, they should be scrubbed and disinfected before use.

Plants

There are conflicting ideas about the use of living plants in terraria, though I personally think that growing one or two plants is well worth the effort, at least in a naturalistic setup. The main problem is that large lizards like the ones discussed in this book tend to be violent and vigorous in their living quarters and are likely to uproot or trample any plants you may put in there. It is best to use only large specimens of tough house plants that can be left in their pots in the terrarium. Keep a couple of sets of plants so you can change them at regular intervals. Species of many of the rubber plants and figs (*Ficus*), dragon trees (*Dracaena*), and umbrella trees (*Schefflera*) have all proved to be reasonably hardy in the terrarium. Pots can be concealed behind roots or cork bark for esthetic purposes.

Backdrops

A variety of landscape backgrounds are commercially available. These can be arranged behind a glass-backed terrarium to give an impression of depth. However, do not commit an esthetic taboo and install an inappropriate picture. A desert scene will hardly complement a pair of water dragons!

WATER

All of the species discussed in this book must have an adequate supply of water in which they can immerse themselves. Water containers can range from plastic cat-litter trays to baby wading pools. Some enthusiasts like to construct natural-looking pools in larger setups. The depth of the water you supply must be at least enough for the lizards to immerse themselves to the shoulders, and preferably deeper so that they can immerse themselves completely. All of the species discussed are good swimmers, but you still must ensure that they have easy access to and from the water, even if this means putting a few rocks in the pool.

The mossy substrate is a good start for keeping these immature green basilisks, but they will need more water than just an artificial backdrop.

THE GUIDE TO OWNING A WATER DRAGON

Getting the Right Environment

Unlike many of the so-called higher animals, reptiles are not very adaptable to environmental conditions different from their own. The climates in which we keep most of our pet water dragons, basilisks, and sailfins are quite different from their jungle or semi-jungle habitats, so we have to try to artificially replicate their natural surroundings as efficiently as possible. The top three considerations for all of the lizards discussed in this book are temperature, lighting, and humidity. A fourth, ventilation, is also covered.

TEMPERATURE

It often is necessary to provide supplementary heating in your pet's enclosure. The recommended temperatures for most of the year (which will be slightly higher when a breeding response is required) are 84 to 88°F during the day, reduced to 75 to 80°F at night. This nighttime temperature reduction is important—reptiles kept permanently in the upper range will not thrive!

A number of heating options are available, including heating pads placed beneath the terrarium, heating cables placed in the substrate, and heated rocks. Ask the assistants at your local pet shop to show you their selection of products. Aquarium heaters immersed in the pool are ideal for maintaining humidity as well as keeping the water warm. This sometimes is important since lizards entering excessively cold water are liable to chill. All heating apparatuses should be used in conjunction with a thermostat to ensure that the correct temperature is maintained. It is sensible to have a thermometer in the terrarium so that you can regularly check the temperature and ensure that the heaters are functioning properly. An efficient way of controlling the day/night temperature fluctuation is to use two thermostats and a timer. One

Large rocks on the sides of a pool simulate the natural habitat of the green water dragon and make a healthy specimen feel at home.

thermostat is set to the daytime temperature range and the other to the nighttime temperature range while the timer is set to turn one off and the other on in the evening and vice versa in the morning.

In addition to the atmospheric heating, your lizards will require specific basking heat. They may use heat rocks if you provide them, but spot lamps are probably better as they give the lizards the illusion that they are basking under an overhead "sun." You can now buy such lamps in many pet shops. These should be used with care, however, for if you place the bulb too close to your lizards or live plants they will be burned. You should experiment by placing a thermometer at the basking spot and raising and lowering the lamp until you find the right temperature. It is advisable to use the basking lamp for only six or seven hours in the middle of the day. Place it at one end of the terrarium so the lizards can cool off at the other end if they so desire. Always ensure that the lizards cannot come into direct contact with the lamp, otherwise they are likely to burn themselves.

LIGHTING

Photoperiod (length of daylight) is as important to our lizards as the correct temperature. We must provide them with a day/night cycle close to the one they experience in the wild. This is particularly important during the breeding season, when photoperiod plays an essential role in reproductive behavior. During most of the year we can maintain a day/night cycle of 12 hours of light and 12 hours of darkness.

Direct sunlight would be ideal, but the provision of this in a glass enclosure poses problems unless the enclosure is portable and can be placed outdoors in suitable weather. In such cases, only sunlight through a mesh screen will be advantageous. Sunlight through glass is not only less beneficial than direct sunlight, it can also pose the problem of overheating the cage. Thus, you usually will have to resort to artificial lighting. There are some excellent fluorescent lamps on the market that provide a very broad spectrum of light, including sufficient ultraviolet. These not only are beneficial to the health of the lizards and plants, but also help to accentuate their colors. Simple ultraviolet lamps (blacklights) once were thought to be beneficial to captive lizards, but they have now proven to be more dangerous than anything else. Prolonged exposure to such rays can cause skin and eye damage. It is thus best to rely on the mild ultravio-

let content of full-spectrum bulbs rather than apply ultraviolet waves in concentration. We can install our lighting to work in conjunction with the heating, and for the most accurate results the lights should be operated with a timer.

HUMIDITY

There is evidence to suggest that seasonal levels of humidity are an important influence on the life cycles of many lizards, particularly those that are native to areas affected by monsoon rains. Basilisks in particular require an increase in relative humidity if they are to be bred. Humidity in the terrarium can be increased by using aquarium heaters in the water body, by using living plants, and by regular mist spraying. A small mist sprayer of the type sold in garden centers should be part of every serious herpetoculturist's basic

Green water dragons, like many lizards, rely on photoperiod to set the time for mating. The longer hours of light after they come out of a cool winter period help adjust reproductive organ development in the lizards and produce successful mating.

equipment. Always use lukewarm water for mist spraying, as cold water can temporarily reduce the terrarium's overall temperature.

VENTILATION

It is important for the air in a terrarium not to become stagnant and stale. Such conditions can induce stress to the occupants of the cage and are an invitation for disease organisms to thrive. However, ventilation in cool areas can cause cold drafts to enter the enclosure, also causing health problems for the occupants. Enclosures should be placed where they are not subjected to such drafts. On the other hand, summer breezes can be beneficial. In most cases, provided you have adequate vents in the terrarium, efficient air change will be promoted by convection arising from the heating apparatus; as the heated terrarium air rises it will be replaced by fresh air from outside.

SAFETY PRECAUTIONS

It should not be necessary to pose a warning, but I will anyway! Most of the environmental systems in your pet's terrarium are operated electrically. Electricity and water in particular are a dangerous combination, so use only apparatus that has passed sensible safety standards. If you are not sure about the efficiency of the wiring, get a qualified electrician to do it for you. A little extra expense may prevent a nasty accident from occurring somewhere down the line.

What's on the Menu?

Before discussing the food items of water dragons, basilisks, and sailfins, let's first have a look at nutrition in general. Nutrition can be thought of as a science that involves the study of growth, maintenance, and repair of the living body in conjunction with the intake of food. Our lizard subjects range from being strictly carnivorous to partially herbivorous (omnivorous). To keep ourselves healthy and to function properly, we are continually reminded that we need a balanced diet, and captive lizards are no different. A balanced diet is one that contains both macronutrients and micronutrients.

Macronutrients include:

Carbohydrates, to provide the body with energy. Excessive carbohydrates are converted into fats. They are obtained mainly from vegetable matter.

Fats, which also provide energy and act as an emergency source of energy in stored body fat. They are obtained prima-rily from animal matter but also occur as plant oils.

Proteins, which are the body's building materials, required for growth and repair and maintenance of tissues as well as other biological functions. They occur in both animal and plant materials but are most readily available in the former.

Micronutrients are essentially:

Vitamins, used to regulate the body processes (metabolism). Vitamins A, B1, B2 complex, D3, and E are probably the most important in reptiles. Although required in minute quantities, a deficiency (known as hypovitaminosis) will cause serious problems, as may an excess (hyper-vitaminosis). A varied diet is one of the keys to providing the proper amounts of vitamins. Technically vitamins are not "burned" or metabolized as are true nutrients, but instead they are catalysts allowing certain chemical reactions to occur or to progress at certain speeds.

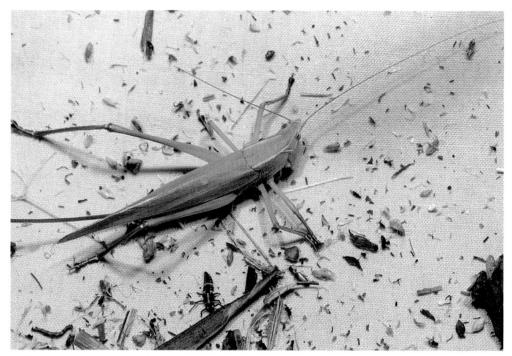

Collecting your own insect foods in season is an excellent idea as it provides your lizard with variety in its diet and reduces the chance of vitamin or mineral shortages.

Mineral salts, particularly those containing calcium and phosphorus. They are essential for bone growth and repair. Compounds containing such elements as sodium, potassium, iron, magnesium, sulfur, and fluorine all are important as constituents of body cells as well as being involved in basic metabolism.

This may all seem complicated, but a balanced diet can be achieved by simply offering as great a variety of foodstuffs as possible. Each item will contain some or all of the basic constituents, but by offering a variety of items we ensure that our lizards are getting what they require.

FOOD ITEMS

The scope of the diet of wild water dragons, basilisks, and sailfin lizards is enormous, and it would be impossible for us to supply the same variety of items in captive conditions. However, by supplying the widest variety of food items possible we will ensure the good health of our lizards.

COLLECTING LIVEFOODS

Many enthusiasts who live in country surroundings will be able to collect a variety of invertebrate livefoods for their animals. Such livefoods will provide supplements to your pet's ordinary diet of cultivated livefoods and vegetable matter. Caterpillars (not the hairy kinds), grasshoppers, crickets, beetles, and spiders can be found in grass and foliage. Some invertebrates, such as woodlice and earthworms, can be dug from the soil or found under rocks, logs, and other ground litter.

Large green grasshoppers are a preferred prey of captive water dragons and basilisks. In the United States these must almost always be wild-collected, but they generally are easy to find during summer and autumn.

Commercially produced crickets often are a mainstay of the diet of smaller water dragons and basilisks, but they should never be the only food offered, even during winter.

Though mealworms are chitinous and sometimes hard to digest, they are readily taken by dragons and basilisks, who tend to chew them well before swallowing.

A good method of catching a variety of terrestrial insects is to use a net. A large net, similar to a butterfly net, swept through the grass and foliage usually will provide an interesting array of creatures. Nocturnal moths, a particularly valuable food item, can be collected during the warmer parts of the year by using a light trap, a light (incandescent, fluorescent, mercury vapor, or ultraviolet) aimed at a white sheet or similar background. Such a trap will attract many moths, which can easily be caught in a net or fingers and transferred to holding containers.

CULTIVATED LIVEFOODS

A number of cultivated livefoods now are available, and it is usually quite easy to buy a selection of these from pet shops.

Crickets: These rapidly are becoming the staple diet for many insectivorous amphibians and reptiles in captivity. Commercial cricket farms now are producing millions of crickets to supply the pet trade. Crickets are considered a very nutritious item, and most lizards will accept them readily. Another advantage of crickets as food is that they can be obtained in various sizes, giving you a varied supply for different-sized lizards. They also are relatively easy to keep. Depending on the species, crickets reach a maximum size of about 1.25 inches.

Crickets can be kept in large, escape-proof containers with ventilation grids. A plastic tub with a mesh-covered hole in the lid is ideal. Place crumpled newspaper in the base to provide hiding places for the insects. Feed them on a fresh mixture of vitamin-supplemented bran and oatmeal, plus green food (dandelion, clover, or romaine lettuce). Pieces of apple or orange will provide enough moisture.

If you want to breed crickets you must maintain them at 77 to 84°F and provide them with dishes of moist sand or vermiculite so they can lay their eggs.

Mealworms: These are another commonly cultivated livefood. Mealworms have lost some popularity in recent times because they are said to be deficient in certain minerals. However, used moderately and with additional vitamin/mineral supplements, they still are a useful item to have around, especially for juvenile lizards.

Mealworms are easy to maintain and propagate, though they are somewhat slow to reproduce. Place about 50 mealworms in a shallow plastic box containing a 2-inch layer of bran or oatmeal into which a little powdered vitamin/mineral supplement has been mixed. Cover the layer with a piece of coarse cloth or burlap, onto which you should place a few pieces of carrot, apple, or potato to provide moisture; change this regularly before it spoils. The box should be covered with a partially ventilated lid and maintained at a temperature of 77 to 84°F. The larvae will grow, pupate, and emerge as adult beetles in about three to five months, then these beetles can be used to start another culture. It is best to have about four cultures going at any one time, dismantling the first culture each time you start a new one (about once per month). This will give you a regular supply.

Grasshoppers: Migratory locusts are large (to 3 inches) insects that make an

In nature green water dragons are mostly carnivorous, so large immatures and adults often take mice in captivity.

All dragons and basilisks will take some vegetable foods, especially when young, but sailfins require the diet to be nearly half vegetables at all ages if they are to remain healthy.

ideal food for larger lizards. Their various nymphal instars are suitable for juveniles. They often are available from livefood suppliers in Europe but cannot be shipped within the U.S. They can be propagated in a glass-fronted cage measuring about 24 x 15 x 15 inches (roughly the size of a 20-gallon aquarium) and warmed with a light bulb from above. Place some twigs in the cage for climbing. They may be fed with bran, oatmeal, and greens placed in a shallow dish. The locusts will lay their eggs in containers filled with a 2-inch layer of sand and peat mixture. For best results, maintain the culture at about 85°F.

Many native North American grasshoppers are easily collected and maintained under somewhat similar conditions, though those from the eastern United States will prefer more humid, somewhat cooler conditions. Some will breed readily in the home, laying their packets of eggs in damp sand. Unfortunately, many have only two generations a year and do not mature until July to September.

Mice: Newborn mice (pinkies) are ideal for our lizards that are large enough to take them. Larger lizards will be able to take fuzzy mice (mice that have grown somewhat and have developed their first fur). Mice can be obtained from most pet shops. If reared on a balanced diet including not only commercial mouse pellets but also seeds of various types and some greens, mice will be highly nutritious for your lizards.

VEGETABLE FOODS

All of the lizards discussed in this book

may take vegetable foods as part of their diet. This includes greens (especially shredded green lettuce, dandelion leaves, and brightly colored flowers) and fruit (especially strawberries, bananas, and melons, as well as most tropical fruits). Adult sailfin lizards in particular need their diet to be about 50% vegetable matter.

VITAMIN AND MINERAL SUPPLEMENTS

To ensure that your lizards are receiving a balanced diet, it is highly recommended that you treat food items with a good vitamin/mineral supplement every few days for juveniles and once per week or two weeks for adults. Powdered reptile supplements (available at many pet shops) can be sprinkled over the food and added to the diet of feeder insects.

Calcium is especially important for juveniles and gravid females.

FEEDING STRATEGIES

Adult water dragons, basilisks, and sailfin lizards should be fed a variety of large livefoods every three or four days, plus a mixture of fruits and vegetables. Some lizards will refuse certain foods, but try various items until you have developed a feeding strategy. Livefood meals commonly are alternated with veggie meals.

Hatchling lizards of all species should be fed daily. The best items are invertebrates such as small mealworms, early instar crickets, small collected insects and spiders, and similar prey. Increase the size of the food items and introduce fruits and vegetables as the lizards grow.

Though the diet should never be based on mice, these rodents are a nice treat for many large basilisks and dragons in terraria. Insects are a more natural food.

A healthy adult green water dragon is a truly spectacular sight, but it takes excellent care for your small pet to reach this stage. As for all large lizards, the keeper must be patient and consistent in all aspects of captive care of dragons and basilisks.

General Care

Anyone keeping animals of any sort must realize that the animals totally rely on them for their welfare. As a rule, water dragons, basilisks, and sailfin lizards will respond well to proper care, but this can only be achieved by dedication and ongoing enthusiasm for your charges. If you don't think you'll be able to maintain this enthusiasm, then keeping terrarium animals is not for you!

One of the most important aspects of terrarium keeping is hygiene—keeping organisms healthy and free of disease. This includes cleanliness, of course, as well as other aspects of general care that will keep your animals in peak condition.

ACQUIRING SPECIMENS

It is essential that any new stock you acquire be healthy and disease-free from the outset. You certainly don't want to have to deal with medical problems at an early stage of your hobby (or at any stage, for that matter).

The most logical place from which to obtain specimens is a pet shop. Captive-bred specimens are preferable to wild-caught because they will settle more easily into captive surroundings than will wild-caught stock since the latter often is stressed after capture, transport, and ensuing confinement. Unfortunately, except for Green Basilisks and the occasional Green Water Dragon, few of these lizards are captive-bred. You may have to be satisfied with calm wild-caught specimens in great physical condition. Don't buy the first animal you see, and don't think you can nurse a specimen back from the edge of death.

It is advisable to purchase specimens only from caring and conscientious dealers who display their wares in clean terraria. Avoid stores that keep their animals in dirty, overcrowded conditions. Don't be overly harsh in your judgment, however. Remember that even the most meticulously run pet shop may have a little dirt; in the pet business this is unavoidable. Your decision must be based on a rational blend of both scrutiny and understanding. Examine each prospective purchase carefully for signs of disease. Healthy specimens will be alert, plump, bright-eyed, free of any wounds or other blemishes on the body, and feeding regularly.

HANDLING

Water dragons, basilisks, and sailfin lizards generally do not like being handled, though some will become tame enough to sit on your arm or shoulder. Even so, you should not do this out of doors because a boisterous lizard may take a sudden liking to its apparent freedom and take off like a shot. All of these lizards are quite speedy and agile (especially when young), so you will have quite a job recapturing them if they get away from you. It is best to avoid handling nervous specimens (such as most juvenile Green Water Dragons) in the first place since they are likely to become highly stressed.

It occasionally will be necessary for you to restrain a lizard for purposes of examination. All the lizards discussed here are quite capable of delivering painful bites, especially large males. Their jaws are strong and their teeth are sharp enough to give you a very ugly wound. They also have long claws and strong tails. Great care must be taken when handling them. Remember that a good herpetoculturist tries to never be bitten by his animals.

A young specimen usually can be picked up gently but firmly with one hand around the body, restraining the neck with your thumb and forefinger to stop it from turning around to bite. Larger lizards should be restrained with one hand around the neck while the other hand is restraining the hind legs and tail. Large specimens can cause deep scratches with their sharp claws and lash with the rough tail. Finally, of course, a lizard should never be picked up by the tail.

TRANSPORT

Once you have bought your lizard, get it home as soon as possible. You should already have its housing ready; don't go out and buy a lizard before you have a proper place to keep it. For carrying, a lizard usually is placed in a cloth bag such as a pillow case. It can breathe through the material of the bag, and the fact that it cannot see through the material of the bag should keep it calm. The cloth also stops the lizard from injuring itself if it gets restless. In cold weather it is wise to place the lizard in some kind of insulated box such as a Styrofoam cooler. Never leave your lizard in direct sunlight or in a parked car during hot or cold weather—a closed car rapidly becomes a death chamber.

QUARANTINE

If you already own some lizards, it is wise not to put any new specimen with them until you are sure of the newcomer's good

Though some adult green water dragons do not dislike being handled, it probably is less stressful to keep human contact to a minimum.

health. It is highly recommended that all new stock first be placed in quarantine.

A quarantine cage can be a small terrarium in which you have all the necessary environmental controls but a minimum of decorations. Keep and feed the lizard in this setup for a couple of weeks, and if it seems healthy you then can introduce it to your other stock. Bringing the lizard to a competent reptile veterinarian for an initial checkup is not a bad idea, but unfortunately reptile vets still are hard to find.

MAINTENANCE OF THE ENCLOSURE

Enclosures must be kept clean. Remove any feces from the substrate with a small scoop. Since most of the lizards discussed in this book tend to defecate in their water (quite often just after you have cleaned it out!), the water must be changed frequently. Keep the terrarium glass sparkling clean. There is nothing more unpleasant-looking than a smeared viewing panel!

Substrate material should be changed at regular intervals. You can use the soiled material in your garden if you've got one. Rocks and branches also should be scrubbed and disinfected or replaced when necessary. The best type of disinfectant is a homemade solution of 5% household beach and 95% water, which must be thoroughly rinsed away with clean, cold water. About once every month you should remove the contents of the terrarium (have a temporary enclosure ready) and give it a thorough cleaning. This also will be the time to make any repairs or modifications to the setup.

HEALTH PROBLEMS

Many veterinarians are versed in reptile medicine, but they still are in a minority and often hard to find. Even if your local vet is not a reptile specialist, he or she may be able to put you in touch with one who is. Your pet shop may be able to tell you of a local vet with reptile interests.

Some of the more usual problems and tips on their treatment are given below.

External Parasites: Newly imported specimens often are infested with a few to many ticks. These unpleasant creatures, which can reach more than a quarter inch in length, attach themselves to the lizard's skin with their piercing mouthparts and feed on the animal's blood. Ticks often are hidden on areas of the body such as the groin, around the neck, and in the loose skin below the neck. Small ones often are embedded under scales of the belly and tail. Ticks can be removed by first dabbing them with alcohol to relax their mouthparts and then gently pulling them out with forceps (tweezers) in a slight clockwise twist.

A mite problem is a bit more serious than a tick problem. Mites are smaller than a pinhead and can breed rapidly. A few mites that have come in with new stock can quickly turn into a large infestation if you are not vigilant. Mites can cause skin problems, stress, and anemia. A mite-infested terrarium should be stripped of all components and disinfected. In some cases an insecticide-impregnated "pest strip" can be used, though some people believe them to be dangerous. A quarter-inch square of the strip is hung from the top of a hospital enclosure in a perforated container (such as a film canister or medicine bottle) so the lizard cannot come into contact with it. After three days the strip is removed. Repeat the process ten days later to kill off any

Ticks, both large and small, are to be expected on wild-caught dragons and basilisks. All new imports must be examined for these pests.

Water dragons and basilisks are prone to nutritional deficiencies if not given a good diet supplemented with vitamins and minerals on a regular basis. A captive diet can never equal one in the wild.

mites that escaped the first treatment. Remove the water bowl during these treatments and also remove all substrate and decorations from the terrarium and sanitize them thoroughly to remove eggs. Mite medicines from the pet shop may or may not work—be sure to follow instructions exactly.

Shedding Difficulties: Healthy lizards shed their skin at regular intervals depending on growth rate. The skin usually is shed in patches, and the entire process should be completed within a few days. Difficulties may arise as the result of a mite infestation or if the lizards are kept in an environment that is too dry. In such cases the skin is shed only partially, with persistent patches remaining. If these are not removed, an infection may result, possibly causing permanent skin damage. The condition usually can be alleviated by immersing the affected lizard in lukewarm water for up to an hour. The skin usually will float away or at the very least will be easier for the lizard to peel off.

Internal Parasites: Various types of internal parasites can infest captive lizards. While the relationship between many worms and their hosts generally is symbiotic, some worms can become a danger to the host in times of stress. Veterinary laboratories can test feces for evidence of worms, and positive cases can be cured by the administration of an appropriate vermicide by your veterinarian.

Nutritional Deficiencies: These often are related to a lack of variety in the diet. Calcium deficiency can be a serious problem for lizards. A lack of calcium manifests itself in, among other things, soft bones, especially those in the lower jaw (which can cause further feeding difficulties). Advanced cases result in severe osteodystrophy (abnormal bone growth). Such disabilities are easily avoided by providing as varied a diet as possible right from the outset, this including a regular vitamin/mineral supplement.

Articular Gout: This was at one time a common disease of many captive lizards. It manifests itself as hard swellings, usually in the limb joints or digits. It arises as a result of excessive urea deposited in the joints, causing irritation and the buildup of scar tissue. The disease usually is triggered by an excess of protein in the diet combined with the inability of the animal to metabolize it efficiently, sometimes due to an inadequate supply of drinking water.

Skin Wounds: The most common type of skin wound seen on the lizards discussed in this book is a damaged snout caused by rubbing or impaction. It occurs when nervous animals continually run into the glass or sides of the terrarium. It often takes a long time for wild-caught specimens to get used to confinement, so it is important that you give them time to calm down. Captive-bred lizards are much less calm and thus less susceptible. In severe cases, such a wound can become infected, resulting in further problems. Treatment includes the swabbing of the infected area with an antiseptic solution and subsequent administration of an appropriate antibiotic. Your veterinarian should be consulted when dealing with particularly bad cases. Repeated banging into the walls and lid may result in breakage or erosion of the snout bones, which cannot be fixed.

Enteric Diseases: Digestive tract infections may be caused by various bacteria, protozoans, or other organisms. An infected specimen will become lethargic, refuse to feed, and lose weight. A further sign is watery or abnormally colored droppings. Fortunately many of these diseases can be successfully treated with veterinary attention.

Respiratory Infections: While relatively uncommon, infections of the lungs in lizards can be severe. Unfortunately, they often go unnoticed until they have developed beyond the point of simple treatment. Symptoms include difficulty in breathing, lethargy, loss of appetite, and gaping of the mouth. Patients should be removed to a dry terrarium (with a small dish of water for drinking) and maintained at a temperature of about 88°F for three or four days. Veterinary antibiotic treatment may be required.

Index

Page numbers in **boldface** indicate photos

Photo Credits

Aqua Press, MP. & C. Piednoir: 13
Randall D. Babb: 33; 36 top
Marian Bacon: 4
R. D. Bartlett: 6 bottom; 15 bottom; 27
Allan Both: 6 top; 8; 16; 34; 37
Walter J. Brown: 24
Matthew Campbell: 40
Isabelle Francais: 1 (Physignathus cocincinus); 44
Paul Freed: 28; 42 bottom; 56; 60
U. Erich Friese: 7; 19; 46; 54
James E. Gerholdt: 36 bottom; 51 bottom
Vladislav T. Jirousek: 22
Erik Loza: 29

Sean McKeown: 18; 31 top; 32 bottom; 47
Gerald & Cindy Merker; 41; 51 top
Gerald L. Moore: 5; 10; 12; 59
John C. Murphy: 31 bottom; 32 top; 35
Aaron Norman: 25; 55; 61
Wayne Rogers: 15 top; 26; 30
Mark Smith: 53
Robert G. Sprackland: 17; 42 top
Karl H. Switak: 11; 14
John C. Tyson: 3 (Physignathus cocincinus)
Maleta Walls: 50
David J. Zoffer: 52